The Lemming Dilemma

Livin~

Leadi~

by D~

illustrat~

PEGASUS COMMUNICATIONS, INC.
Waltham

The Lemming Dilemma: Living with Purpose, Leading with Vision
by David Hutchens; illustrated by Bobby Gombert
Copyright © 2000 by David Hutchens
Illustrations © Pegasus Communications

Library of Congress Cataloging-in-Publication Data
Hutchens, David, 1967–
The lemming dilemma: Living with purpose, leading with vision /
by David Hutchens ; illustrated by Bobby Gombert. –1st ed.
p.   cm.
ISBN 1-883823-45-5
Organizational learning. 2. Management. I. Title
HD58.82.H8   2000
658.4—dc21   99-36522
CIP

Acquiring editor: Kellie Wardman O'Reilly
Project editor: Lauren Keller Johnson
Production: Nancy Daugherty

♻ Printed on recycled paper.
Printed in the United States of America.
First edition. First printing January 2000.

The Lemming Dilemma
Volume Discount Schedule
1–4 copies $19.95 each • 50–149 copies $13.97 each
5–19 copies $17.96 each • 150–299 copies $11.97 each
20–49 copies $15.96 each • 300+ copies $9.98 each
Prices and discounts are subject to change without notice.

Pegasus Communications, Inc.
One Moody Street
Waltham, MA 02453-5339
www.pegasuscom.com
Phone: (781) 398-9700
Fax: (781) 894-7175

05 04 03 02 01 00   10 9 8 7 6 5 4 3 2 1

For Emory,
who brings me clarity

Please note that no actual lemmings or management consultants were in any way hurt, mistreated, or even verbally maligned during the development of this story. The author voluntarily observes full compliance with the guidelines of the ASPCC (American Society for the Prevention of Cruelty to Consultants).

Chapter 1:
Lemmings 101

These are lemmings.

This is a tall cliff.

(If you know where this is heading and you have a weak stomach, you may wish to skip the next few pages.)

Oh the horror.

Yes, lemmings jump off cliffs.

Why do they do this? No one really knows. Some scientists, having nothing better to do, have puzzled over this question for decades.

Maybe this behavior is instinctual. Maybe it's culturally conditioned. Whatever the answer, thousands of lemmings the world over continue to march to the edges of cliffs and simply leap into the great unknown.

Among lemmings, this behavior is considered normal.

Take, for example, the annual "Great Lemming JumpFest." Rarely witnessed by scientists, this eagerly anticipated event features dancing, barbecue, and Elvis impersonations, and culminates in the "Big Leap."

Lemmings never think about
why they jump off cliffs.

They just do it.

Chapter 2:
Enough
Introduction—
Let's Get on with
the Story

This is Emmy.

Emmy grew up with a bunch of other lemmings among the rubber trees and crabgrass, just a few miles from the edge of a cliff.

These were days filled with laughter and joy.

But as Emmy became older, she, like all the others, began to feel the strange pull toward the edge of the cliff.

All the other lemmings chattered excitedly about the coming "Great Lemming JumpFest," and many of Emmy's young friends were even planning to participate this year.

But Emmy was troubled. One day, she decided to talk with her friends about the Big Leap.

"Why do we jump off the cliff?" Emmy asked them.

"What do you mean, *why?* We're lemmings. It's what we're *supposed* to do, silly," her friends answered.

"Yes, but what happens after we go over the edge?" she pressed.

"Something good."

"What?"

"...We don't know," came the hesitant response.

"Then how do you know it's good?" Emmy insisted, noting a hint of fear in their voices.

Her friends fell quiet. Finally, one of them said, "It *must* be good, because no one ever comes back."

"That's right," the others agreed in relief. "Now *please* shut up."

Emmy wasn't satisfied. The next day, she went to speak with the wise elders of the herd.

"Good morning, young lady," said the wise elders. "What may we do for you?"

"I came to find out why lemmings jump off the cliff," Emmy replied.

"Why, that's a mighty big question for such a little lemming," said one, peering over his glasses at her. "Do you have a problem with jumping off the cliff?"

"I don't know. At least, I don't *think* so. Maybe I'd feel better about it if I just knew why we did it—or *why* we do *anything*, for that matter."

The elders nodded their furry little heads. "We understand your concern," they said. "That's why we have flown in a high-priced management consultant, Hans, to help us write a purpose statement for all of the lemmings."

"Hi there!" grinned Hans, grabbing Emmy's paw and shaking it vigorously.

"In fact," the elders continued, "we just completed the purpose statement. Here. Read it yourself," they said, handing her a neatly type-set piece of paper.

It said:

> The Lemming Purpose Statement:
> Our purpose is to be value-added
> lemmings pursuing maximization,
> implementation, utilization, and
> blah-blah-blah-ization of total
> quality, excellence, win/win
> customer service, continual
> improvement, et cetera, et cetera.
> But mainly it's to jump off the cliff.

"There. That's your purpose," grinned Hans as he handed his bill to the elders. "Now, no more of this running about asking questions."

Poor little Emmy left feeling more troubled than ever.

That evening, she walked to the very edge of the cliff and sat, dangling her legs over that deep and mysterious abyss.

What's wrong with me that I can't be satisfied with jumping off the cliff like all the others? she wondered. *Am I weird for asking so many questions, and for wanting something else?*

What do I want, anyway?

Who am I? Why am I here?

Emmy sat there alone, crying and gazing at the far side of the canyon for a long, long time.

Chapter 3:
The Resistance

A few days later, as Emmy was resting beneath the shade of a giant rubber-tree leaf, she heard a voice.

"Psssst!"

"Who's there?" she asked, looking around. Standing behind her was another young lemming.

"Hi. I'm Lenny," he whispered.

"Well, hello," she said, surprised. "Pleased to meet you."

"Shh! Not so loud," Lenny said, looking about nervously. "Let me get to the point. I hear you've been asking questions. I hear you don't want to take the Big Leap."

"I don't know," Emmy said, taken aback. "I'm trying to figure out what I want."

"What if I could introduce you to other lemmings— lemmings like you?"

"Lemmings like *me?*" she asked eagerly.

"Yes—lemmings who don't want to jump. Follow me!"

And with that, he disappeared into the bushes. Her heart pounding, she quickly followed him.

Lenny led her to a hole in the ground and jumped in. They followed an underground tunnel for a short distance, until it opened into a small cave. There, seated in a circle, were seven or eight other lemmings.

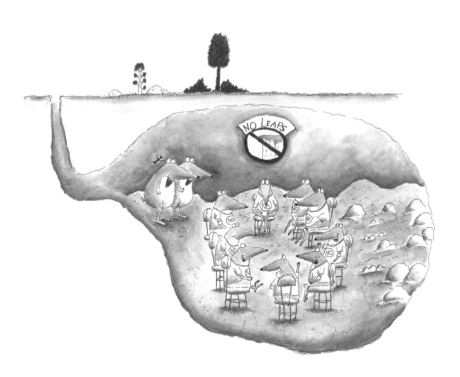

"Hi, everyone," said Lenny. "This is Emmy."

"Hi, Emmy!" everyone said in unison.

"Welcome," said the lemming sitting at the front of the group. "My name is Fleming. And we are the N.O. L.E.A.P.S.—The New Order of Lemmings for an Earthbound and Moderate Society." (It occurred to Emmy that this actually produced the acronym "NO LEAMS"... but not wishing to seem like a know-it-all, she kept this observation to herself.)

"Are you here to join our group?" continued Fleming.

"I ... I'm not sure," Emmy replied. "What's the purpose of the N.O. L.E.A.P.S?"

"Our purpose? Well, we don't want to jump off the cliff," said Fleming.

"Oh," said Emmy politely. "I can see that's what you *don't* want. But ... what is it that you *do* want?"

"What we do want," Fleming said, puzzled, "is ... to avoid jumping."

"I see," sighed Emmy, beginning to worry that her questions were bordering on rudeness. Yet something was bothering her about the conversation. The N.O. L.E.A.P.S.' reasons for existing as a group all seemed so ... well, *negative.* She tried to imagine what a more positive-sounding purpose might sound like. Taking a deep breath, she pressed on: "But what is it that you want to ... to ... *add* to the world, or *create?*" Emmy asked.

"We want to create … a society that doesn't jump," said Fleming, tiring of this little game. "Now please, pull up a seat," she added sternly. "Our meeting is about to begin. Tonight we're planning our protest demonstration for the Great Lemming JumpFest."

Emmy sat down next to Lenny. Although she was happy to have met such nice lemmings, she still felt confused and sad.

It seems like most lemmings jump off the cliff without ever thinking about why they're doing it, why they exist, or what they want to create with their lives, she thought to herself.

And these guys only seem to think about what they don't want.

I'm not sure which way of living would be worse.

At that moment, Emmy decided she would no longer look to others to tell her who she should be or what she should do with her life.

She would just have to figure these things out for herself.

Chapter 4:
Clarity for
Emmy

It was a lovely, autumn day—the kind of day that made you just want to go jump off a cliff (if you were a lemming).

But as her friends all played together, Emmy found herself once again drawn to the cliff edge, where she sat gazing at the other side of the canyon.

Far in the distance, she noticed a single, tall tree growing on the other side. She had never seen a tree like it, so tall and sturdy. *What else is out there?* she wondered. *What kind of world exists beyond our meadow? What possibilities are out there for us— possibilities that we've never seen?*

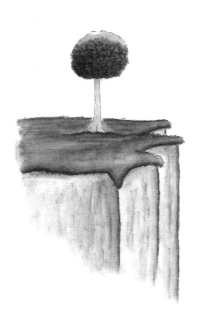

"Hi, Emmy," came a voice from behind her.

Emmy turned. "Hi, Lenny!" she said, startled but delighted.

"I haven't seen you since the N.O. L.E.A.P.S. meeting a few weeks ago," he said. "I've been worried about you."

"I've been taking time to think," she replied, staring down at her feet.

"Me too," Lenny replied. "I've been thinking about those questions you asked at the meeting. Like when you asked *what is our purpose* and *what is it we want to create?*"

"Oh," she said, looking away. "I hope I didn't embarrass you in front of your friends."

"No. They were great questions. I've never heard any of the lemmings ask them before. Do you mind if I sit with you?"

"Please, do," she said.

Lenny took a seat next to Emmy, and together they gazed out over the canyon.

"Emmy?" said Lenny after a long silence.

"Yes?"

"What is *your* purpose?"

Emmy thought for a moment.

"It has nothing to do with jumping," she finally replied, "or even *not* jumping."

Emmy's eyes were drawn again to that tall tree, so far away. She continued: "I'm starting to think my purpose has something to do with *asking questions*— questions that can open up whatever bigger world is beyond our little meadow and help us see new ways of being. I can't explain why, but this just seems to be part of who I am. I think that may be my purpose."

She thought some more. "The more I understand who I am, the more it makes me want to *do* something— something special. So I've been asking myself *what do I really want to create?*

"I … I guess all of this must sound kind of intense," Emmy concluded.

"Well … y-yes," said Lenny, who now had a headache.

Emmy looked at him apologetically. "I'm beginning to think it can take a long time to figure these things out," she said.

Lenny was deep in thought.

"Ever since you asked those questions at the N.O. L.E.A.P.S. meeting, I've been thinking about *my* purpose," he said. "It might sound silly... but I've always wanted to be a motivational speaker. Does that count as a purpose?"

"I don't know," Emmy replied. Then she asked, "Why does being a motivational speaker interest you?"

Lenny thought hard. "Because I want to motivate lemmings to stop jumping off cliffs, I suppose."

"But why is that so important to you?" she asked.

Lenny sat there silently. This was one of the hardest conversations he had ever had ... and yet, just talking about these things seemed to evoke a strange energy or electricity within him. "I want this because ... I could show the lemmings how much we depend on each other, and how we could find joy in being a community."

Emmy and Lenny looked at each other in surprise. It was amazing how much they could learn about themselves simply by asking *why* they wanted the things they wanted.

Emmy asked again: "Okay. *Why* is being a community so important to you?"

Lenny thought for a long time. "I can't answer why this time," he finally responded. "I want it because I want it."

Emmy tried to summarize Lenny's thoughts. "So your purpose might have something to do with helping all the lemmings find joy in being a community. And one way you could do that would be to become a motivational speaker."

"Yeah," Lenny said. He broke into a big, warm smile as he realized there might be a connection between his purpose and the things he deeply cared about doing.

Suddenly, Lenny knew that he would have to leave the N.O. L.E.A.P.S. It was now so clear to him that their goal wasn't what he wanted, he was surprised that he hadn't seen it before.

"Boy," he said, "it sure is hard to think about this stuff! No wonder most lemmings just jump off the cliff. It's certainly easier than trying to understand yourself!"

Emmy and Lenny both fell silent.

As they sat, Emmy found herself gazing again at the tree on the far side of the canyon. She thought once more about her purpose: *to ask questions that open up bigger worlds, and to see new ways of being.*

All of a sudden, she had a new question to ask: "Lenny, what do you suppose is on the other side of the canyon?"

Lenny shrugged.

Suddenly, Emmy knew what she had to do.

Chapter 5:
The Great Lemming
JumpFest

Several days passed.

Emmy was hard at work.

"Oh, *there* you are, Emmy," said Lenny, rounding the corner of a tree. "Everyone's been asking about you. The Great Lemming JumpFest is tomorrow, you know."

"I know," said Emmy. "I've been working."

"This is your work?" Lenny asked. "It looks like you drew a tree on a rock."

"Not just a tree. I drew it to help me concentrate," she replied.

"And now you're sewing rubber tree leaves together?"

"Mmm hmm," she said.

Lenny didn't know what to say. "So," he stammered, "I hear competition is pretty stiff for the Elvis impersonations at JumpFest this year...."

"That's nice," Emmy said, without looking up from her work. "Say, would you help me gather more rubber tree leaves? Thanks."

Obediently, Lenny began collecting the rubbery leaves.

As he worked, he glanced at Emmy from time to time. *I don't think anything could stop her,* he marveled to himself. *Maybe that's what happens when you figure out what you really want.*

Just think how much the lemmings could accomplish together if each of us knew our purpose, and knew what we wanted to create.

That night, Lenny helped Emmy sew rubber tree leaves together. They worked silently, both lost in their own thoughts, stopping only when the sun peeked above the horizon.

It was morning. JumpFest had begun.

As the sun rose higher into the sky, the meadow began bursting with energy.

"Welcome to the Great Lemming JumpFest!" one of the lemming elders boomed into a bullhorn.

"I'm gonna do a swan dive!" called one lemming.

"I'm gonna do a cannonball!" laughed another.

"Look at that teamwork!" grinned Hans from the buffet table, where he was cramming free barbecue into his mouth.

"Woooooo, wooooo!" screamed the lady lemmings as the Elvis impersonators gyrated and disrobed, throwing scarves and donuts over the edge of the cliff.

"We won't jump! We won't jump!" chanted the N.O. L.E.A.P.S. from the edge of the crowds.

It was time for Emmy to take action.

Lenny helped her slip an elastic cord, sewn from rubber-tree leaves and attached to a sling-shot, around her waist.

Then he wrapped a second one around her, securing it to a stump just behind her.

All Emmy had to do was nibble through the cord holding her back, and she would be shot high above the canyon, to the tree and whatever bigger world waited for her on the opposite side.

Lenny hugged her. "Good luck," he said sadly, realizing at that moment how much he would miss her.

Emmy began nibbling at the release cord.

But then she did something that she never thought she would:

She hesitated.

She looked behind her.

There, she could see the beautiful green meadow where she had grown up. And she could see Lenny, with tears trickling down his face and matting down the fur on his cheeks.

Then she looked before her.

She saw the jagged edge of the cliff, the deep expanse of the canyon, and the tree on the opposite side.

She froze.

The tension around her middle was tremendous, as one elastic cord drew her powerfully toward the uncertainty of her dream, and the other drew her just as powerfully back to safety and comfort.

Emmy burst into tears. "I can't!" she cried. "I can't do it!"

She hung there, suspended, for a long, long time, unable to choose, and barely able to breathe.

"Why does everything have to be so hard?" she asked Lenny in despair. "Why is it that whenever I'm so close to getting what I want, suddenly I start thinking I can't have it?"

"Don't listen to those feelings," Lenny urged her. "They'll ruin everything."

"No," she sighed. "I can't pretend that I don't feel the way I feel. That would make me just like the N.O. L.E.A.P.S."

With this realization, she felt her anxiety lift just a little bit.

"WE WON'T JUMP! WE WON'T JUMP!" came the
chant of the N.O. L.E.A.P.S.

"On your marks … get set … GO!" hollered the
lemming elders as they fired a gun.

"YAHOOOOOOOO!" howled the lemmings as they
raced toward the edge of the cliff.

"I'm inspired!" grinned Hans, spontaneously jumping
over the edge himself.

Even some of the N.O. L.E.A.P.S. could no longer resist the pull, and broke ranks in a mad rush for the edge.

"You have to choose," Lenny whispered to Emmy.

Emmy took a deep breath and began thinking about the things she really wanted.

She looked at the tree.

She looked at Lenny.

Then, she cut the cord.

Soaring over the canyon, Emmy felt the wind roaring through her fur. She maneuvered her arms and legs to steer toward the soft, leafy branches of the tree on the other side.

Then she looked down.

Below she saw the sharp rocks at the foot of the cliff and the awful truth that awaited the falling lemmings. "No!" she gasped. Suddenly she began to hesitate and veer off-course.

Don't look down, she told herself fiercely. *Stay focused on the tree!* She tore her gaze away from the horror below and looked steadfastly at the tree once more.

Her head up, and her arms and legs stretched out, she rode the wind all the way to the other side.

With a soft "whoosh!" Emmy finally landed in the leafy branches of the tree.

She just lay there with her eyes closed. She didn't even feel any need to look around …

… because, in a strange way, the world already seemed much bigger, and full of more possibilities, than she could have ever imagined.

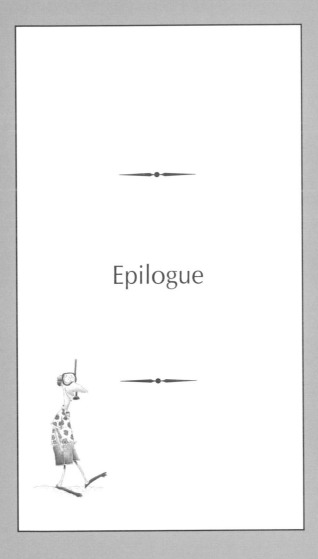

Epilogue

After Emmy's legendary flight across the canyon, nothing was ever the same in the meadow.

Lenny the lemming went on to become a motivational speaker, inspiring the other lemmings to see how valuable their community was and to identify all the unique ways each lemming could contribute to the herd.

With coaching from Lenny, Fleming realized that her purpose was to "enable other Lemmings to explore."

She disbanded the N.O. L.F.A.P.S. and went on to found TransLemming Airways, a transportation conglomerate that flung lemmings en masse from one side of the cliff to the other using the rubber-tree-leaf system pioneered by Emmy.

As more and more inquisitive lemmings tried "flinging," some brought back wonderful new foods and other delights they had discovered from "the other side." This became the foundation of a burgeoning barter economy for the lemmings.

The lemming elders refused to end "The Big Leap," maintaining that it was too important to their heritage and their identity as a group. So every year, many lemmings continued to leap to their deaths.

Still, with help from Lenny, more and more lemmings began to ask "why," and to consider other sources of meaning for their lives.

After hurling himself from the cliff on that fateful day, Hans the consultant suffered a major concussion, permanently damaging the part of the brain that allows consultants to charge exorbitant fees for non-value-added work. Today he is a productive member of society, operating a scuba diving tour boat in Key West, Florida.

And as for Emmy,
she's still asking questions ...

... and discovering bigger worlds
and new ways of being every day.

The End

A Closer Look at *The Lemming Dilemma*

——•——

Who are you? Why do you exist? What is your purpose in the world? What is it you wish to create?

Pretty heady questions for such a simple little story. But on the surface, the questions are quite simple too. The surprising thing is that many people (and many lemmings) live much of their lives without ever considering them at all. That's a shame, because as Emmy and Lenny discovered, there's a lot of power in these questions. Indeed, you'll find that some interesting changes may begin to take place within you simply as a result of reflecting on them. Go ahead and begin considering them now, as you read. Allow the questions to settle into your thoughts. Think about your role in the world, and the things that bring you the strongest sense of meaning and joy.

Who are you? And what is it you wish to create?

Living in 10th Gear

——•——

Imagine that your life is a stationary 10-speed bicycle. Attached to the back wheel of your bike is an electrical generator. As you pedal, the turbine produces energy, which powers a large light bulb just beside you. Now imagine that you are surrounded by many other people on stationary 10-speed bicycles, each with its own generator and light bulb. As you look across this vast landscape of cyclists, you notice that many are pedaling with determination, generating enough energy to produce a nice, even light. You see many other people who are pedaling furiously in first gear—to the point of exhaustion—with nothing to show for their effort but a wavering, weak light.

But you also see a small number pedaling in 10th gear with relative ease, comfortably feeding the powerful torque of the rear wheel, which is now spinning in a blur. These cyclists are producing enough

64

power to brightly light a house, a small neighborhood ... maybe even a city.

Ask Yourself:

- Why do some people expend much effort but produce so few desirable results in their lives?

- If 10th gear is such a desirable state, why isn't *everyone* in 10th gear? What's different about the 10th-gear pedalers?

- *Which cyclist are you?*

The Lemming Dilemma is a story about *personal mastery*—the ability to consistently create the results you want in life with an economy of means. Or, if you like, think of it as living in 10th gear. Practitioners of personal mastery are constantly clarifying their sense of their own unique contribution to the world, continually growing, and, intentionally or not, creating results that elevate the world and people around them.

The Organizational Connection

As discussion of personal mastery has grown within the organizational arena, some people have responded with skepticism: "All of this sounds like one of those 'soft skills' or 'touchy-feely' things," goes a common reaction. "Isn't there more urgent (and measurable) work we could be doing in our organization?"

Those who hold this assumption might remind themselves that organizations are, after all, made up of *individuals*. Likewise, organizations that are highly capable are made up of *highly capable individuals*. Remember Lenny's observation: *"Just think how much the lemmings could accomplish together if we all knew why we existed and what we wanted to create."* The compelling possibility of this discipline is a workforce driven by an inexhaustible, inner motivation that results in endless innovation for the organization.

Like the Lemming elders, many leaders have invested a lot of thoughtful time establishing a company mission or purpose statement in order to align members of the organization. That many of these statements receive a lukewarm and passive reception should come as no surprise. After all, there is no magic in that framed document hanging in the lobby. In fact, such jargony statements frequently fail to capture the essence of why the organization exists. Moreover, they often fail to connect with the aspirations of employees. Today, as many organizational leaders strive for deeper clarity on why they exist as individuals and as an organization, a new awareness is also emerging: People are able to connect wholeheartedly to a higher organizational vision *only when they can see how it is aligned with the things they personally care about most deeply and passionately.*

For organizations, personal mastery is not just an individual concern. It's an issue of *leadership.* By enabling people to explore their own sense of purpose, and by creating an environment that supports the practice of personal mastery, leaders can begin to strengthen alignment between the organization's purpose and the purposes of individual employees. In an age where it is harder and harder to retain dedicated, skilled employees, companies that enable the development of personal mastery (and then seek to align people with a shared vision) have an unparalleled edge in the marketplace. When these mastery skills are addressed at both the organizational and individual levels, an amazing thing occurs: Organizations can experience a shift from a workforce that is merely *compliant* ("I'll do my job because the boss said so") to one that is *enrolled* ("I'm here because I believe in what I am doing and I care enough about it to make it happen").

While there is much more that could be said about shared vision and the *organizational* applications of personal mastery, *The Lemming Dilemma* explores the discipline as it is practiced by *individuals*—one lemming at a time, if you will. At its heart, personal mastery is an intensely private pursuit. Moreover, it doesn't happen by accident. It is a journey of self-awareness that one must choose to take. To begin, all you need to do is stop pedaling, find a quiet place, and take a look deep inside yourself.

Your Life: Form and Structure

Next time you have the opportunity to do so, take a seat at the edge of a river or stream. Note how the water flows and changes, morphing and shifting as it makes its way downstream. The surface may ripple gently, only to settle just a little farther downstream in a smooth, glassy plane that barely seems to be moving at all. Then, just a little farther down, tranquility may break into chaos as the serene surface erupts into a roar of turbulence. Of course, there is little mystery in this; common sense tells us there must be large rocks or fallen trees just beneath the surface, or perhaps the river bed is shallow at certain points. But we often cannot see these submerged, hidden structures; instead, we see only their effects as the surface of the water changes.

Your life is shaped by hidden structures too. You may see a surface that is tranquil or chaotic; the direction of your life may be meandering or straightforward; you might feel a powerful flow of force or a stagnant trickle of movement. But if you look deeper, you'll begin to discover the invisible structures directing the course of your life.

If you reflect on the lemmings' story, you'll find that there were many structures that informed the actions of the lemming herd. The instinct to jump is one structure. So were the herd's cultural pressures and social expectations. The rulings and edicts of the lemming elders were additional structures, as was the lemmings' geographic location near the edge of a cliff. Together, all of these structures conspired to create an environment that made it nearly irresistible for lemmings to jump off a cliff.

As Emmy discovered, new possibilities for shaping our own lives come to light when we expose such structures. It's when we *don't* acknowledge or recognize them that structures begin to hold great power over us.

Structures can be *external*. For example, the behaviors of others can have a very palpable influence on us. Likewise, biology, the law, geography, and even the force of gravity all impose external structures that influence what form our lives may take. But just as often (and perhaps more powerfully), the structures are internal. Some people have psychological scars left by past abuse. Some are blessed with specific capabilities and talents. And we all have self-perceptions and mental models that can be stubbornly difficult to surface and examine. [1]

So, given the power of these structures at work in our lives, how do people ever change?

Let us return to the river for another lesson. Suppose you wanted to create a fish pond fed by the river. To build the pond, you could stand in the river with a bucket and scoop water out, throwing it toward your desired location for the pond. Or maybe, using your hands, you could try to redirect the flow of the water in that direction. But of course these strategies won't work. *You can't change the course of the water by trying to manipulate the water itself.* Instead, you must change the river bed—the structure—perhaps by digging a new trench from the river, and hollowing out some ground for the water to fill.

Sounds logical. But we seldom do this in our lives. Instead, we attempt to manipulate the *form* of our lives—the "surface stuff." If we want to lose weight, we try to stop eating. If we are depressed, we call a friend/go shopping/see a movie, etc. And in the story, the lemmings who wanted to deny their powerful, inborn instinct to jump formed the N.O. L.E.A.P.S. protest group. All of these solutions are like the cyclist pedaling faster and faster to power the light bulb. They are exhausting, reactive strategies that produce hollow, fleeting results. To discover the path to enduring change, we must dig deeper—to the structural level.

For Your Reflection:

- Think of examples of the following kinds of structures that influence your life: *biological/ physiological; economic; geographical; sociological; political; your natural talents and gifts; your limitations;*

[1] This important subject is explored in the Learning Fable titled *Shadows of the Neanderthal: Illuminating the Beliefs That Limit Our Organizations.*

your family experience; the beliefs you have about yourself, your family, your friends, and your colleagues; etc.

• Select two or three structures from the list above. For each, ask:

  – How does this structure influence my life?

  – How does it influence the way I see myself? The way I relate to other people?

  – How does it affect my ability to be effective, and the way I experience the larger world?

(Note: It may be valuable to reflect on these things with someone who knows you well, or with a coach who can ask probing questions.)

Creative Tension: The Core Structure for Change

In his book *The Path of Least Resistance,* author Robert Fritz shows that we break free from the self-defeating and limiting structures in our lives when we create a whole new structure—one that naturally leads us where we want to go. This is what he means by "the path of least resistance." The water follows the river bed, because that's where it is easiest for the energy to flow.

People who are consistently able to create the results they want in their lives with the least expended effort are merely following the path of least resistance.

This is a mind-shifting thought, with startling implications. After all, weren't we always told that the *real* achievers were the ones who were smarter? Tougher? More persistent? Who simply tried harder? Certainly we may find such traits in accomplished people. But such traits are not at the heart of personal mastery. Instead, people with a high degree of personal mastery are adept at creating new structures in their lives that naturally and efficiently draw them where they want to be.

Fritz explains that there is one powerful, core structure that can

69

enable change in your life. This structure can be called *creative tension* (termed *structural tension* by Fritz). Here's how it works. When you begin to clarify your *desired future state*, or *vision*, and also come to a deep awareness of your *current reality*, you create a gap—a space between where you are now and where you want to be. This gap generates tension. Because it is the natural tendency of tension to seek resolution, this gap will seek to close—just like an extended rubber band—and pull you *toward* your vision. (Why doesn't the gap close the opposite way, pulling us *back* toward our current reality? The reason is that a

My desired future state   *My current reality*

vision is a more stable structure than a *current reality*, which is always changing. This is why it's so important for our visions to be clear. Without a strong vision, there's no direction and no tension resolution.)

If it's a new concept to you, creative tension may seem a little strange. But it's really quite natural. Notice how Emmy used creative tension in the story. She was propelled over the cliff not out of sheer willpower but by the resolving tension in a literal rubber band—a graphic metaphor for the force that creative tension carries. For Emmy, this tension resulted from the gap between her current reality of life in the meadow, and her passion for the desired future state of reaching the tree over the canyon.

Even if you are not aware of it, you are already affected by creative tension as you continually change. Like the river, you're going *somewhere*. But by *leveraging* creative tension, you may participate in deciding *where*.

Before we explore ways to put creative tension to work, let's first take a look at the *creative orientation*, and the difference between *reacting* and *creating*.

Reacting Versus Creating

There are two fundamental orientations that influence how we approach life, and why we do the things we do. These are a *reactive orientation* and a *creative orientation*.

Like the N.O. L.E.A.P.S., we often view our place in the world from a reactive orientation, in which we constantly respond to the things we *don't* want. The problem with this orientation is that *it doesn't create anything new*. It simply *gets rid of (or avoids) what is*. This is not all bad. Indeed, if I have a thorn in my foot or ants in my kitchen, a reactive strategy may be appropriate. But practiced as a lifestyle, reacting produces little sustainable leadership, innovation, or constructive meaning.

In contrast, a *creative orientation* poises us for new possibilities, lasting change, and constant adaptability. Note that a "creative orientation" isn't necessarily about "being creative." Rather, it is about entering into that core structure that creates the tension for change. People who approach the world in this way ask a very different set of questions: "What do I want to create? What do I deeply desire to bring into existence?" Despite the fact that Emmy shared the herd's self-defeating instinct to jump, she chose to focus on the things that were of deepest importance to her. The ultimate result was a ripple effect of new possibilities throughout the herd. Such is the product of a *creative orientation*.

As Emmy found, exploring questions such as *Who am I? Why am I here?* enabled a creative-tension structure that carried her to new and exciting worlds. So can you.

For Your Reflection:

- What orientation—creative or reactive—do you notice yourself living in most often (while at work, home, etc.)?

- When you slip into a reactive orientation (one that isn't necessarily called for by the situation), what does it take for you to shift into a creative orientation?

- When do you most typically find yourself in a creative orientation? When you are in a creative orientation, what are your thoughts, feelings, and actions like?

Purpose and Vision

Have you ever admired someone whose life was organized around one central, important thing, and they seemed to have endless energy to devote to it? We tend to regard such people with a degree of envy. But the fact is, they are operating from the same place of purpose and vision that is possible within every one of us. The difference is one of self-knowledge.

Knowing what you really want in life—and why you want it—can be surprisingly difficult. If you struggle with these introspective questions, don't feel foolish. The fact is, self-knowledge is tricky. Confucius, Plato, and the Delphic Oracle all spoke of the difficulty of "knowing thyself." Lenny contemplated this mystery when he said, *"No wonder most lemmings just jump off the cliff. It's certainly easier than trying to understand yourself!"*

The Lemming Dilemma introduces two arenas of self-awareness—*purpose* and *vision*—that are central to the pursuit of personal mastery. These concepts are closely linked yet have some important differences:

PURPOSE	VISION
• Answers the question *"Why* do I exist?"	• Answers the question *"What* do I want to create?"
• Inspires a process of *discovery*; unfolds over time and reveals itself to you as you live your life.	• Catalyzes action, and a process of *imagining, inventing,* and *designing*; is something you choose to bring into existence.
• Is enduring; may remain constant throughout much of your life.	• Changes; you may pursue many different visions during the course of your life.

Let's explore each of these awarenesses in a little more depth.

"Why Do I Exist?": Clarifying Your Purpose

All systems, whether they are biological, mechanical, or organizational, have a basic *purpose* or reason for being. For example, the purpose of the plumbing system in your home is to deliver water to and expel it from the house. The purpose of a tree is to seek sunlight and water, so that it can grow and thrive and contribute to the ecosystem of which it is a part.

Whether it is articulated or not, an organization also exists for a basic purpose: The Walt Disney Company says that theirs is "to make people happy"; The Coca-Cola Company's purpose is "to refresh the world"; NASA states theirs as "advancing man's capability to explore the heavens."

As a human being, *you* are also a system. So it makes sense that you would have a purpose, too. Emmy's purpose, as she came to understand it, was to ask questions that open up new possibilities and new ways of being. Lenny's purpose was to help other lemmings find joy in community.

Purpose is not something you create. Rather, it is something you *discover* as you pay attention to where your life is most fulfilling, and where you find the most joy and meaning. Your task is to seek deeper awareness of your purpose as it unfolds over time.

As you grow more and more aware of your purpose, it can become the element that brings synergy to all areas of your life (including, as we will see, your *visions*). It is the core from where you lead your life. Imagine a life where your job was not *just* a job but an inseparable extension of yourself; where relationships were formed not passively but with a shared intention; where every act of creating was a meaningful expression of self. Purposeful living is energizing. Just as Lenny had a sudden insight that he needed to leave the N.O. L.E.A.P.S., awareness of your purpose leads to clarity in all of your decisions about what to embrace in your life.

73

So, what is *your* purpose, your reason for being? Good question. Only you can answer that.

In thinking about your purpose, it's easy to make the same mistake that Lenny did and confuse ways of *achieving* the purpose with the purpose itself. Lenny originally wondered if his purpose was to be a motivational speaker. Yet he soon realized that he had a deeper purpose: to help lemmings find joy in community. That purpose could indeed be accomplished by his becoming a motivational speaker—and could probably be accomplished through many other means as well. You can begin to discern your purpose in the same way that Emmy and Lenny did: by asking *why* you want the things you want. For example, suppose you want to run your own business, or publish a book, or have a large family. That's fine. But what is it about those things that is enticing to you? If you achieved any of these, what would it get you? *Why* is it important to you? Continually digging deeper in this way will help you clarify your sense of purpose.

For Your Reflection:

- Imagine that you have a unique purpose that is fulfilled by everything you are and everything you do. What do you think that purpose is?

- To begin exploring your life purpose, consider:

  - taking a private retreat to reflect.

  - talking with a friend or mentor who you see as having a clear sense of his or her own purpose.

  - recalling events and activities in your life that are deeply meaningful to you. Are there some common themes to these events? How might these themes point you toward a deeper awareness of your purpose?

74

"What Do I Want to Create?":
The Defining Characteristics of Vision

Let's now shift our focus from *purpose* to the realm of action: the definition of *vision*, or desired future state. Just as Emmy aimed for the tree on the other side of the canyon, we must be very clear about what we want in order for the creative-tension structure to propel us forward. The specifics of the vision are up to you; however, an effective vision does have certain characteristics.

- **It is specific and clearly recognizable.** A vision is specific enough that you say, "Ah-hah! That's it!" when you either visualize or achieve it. A desire to "get people in my organization to have more of a social conscience" does not have the same power or clarity as a vision of "a program to partner members of my company in mentoring relationships with troubled, inner-city children." Likewise, someone who has a vision to live in a calm, serene, and inviting home will certainly know it when they have achieved that vision.

- **It is something you *want*—not something you *don't want*.** This idea is both simple and profound. Many diets fail because we're focused on the thing we *don't* want. ("I don't want that spare tire around my middle.") Likewise, many people define their visions as the N.O. L.E.A.P.S. did: existing to get rid of something, whether it is the Lemming JumpFest, debt, a boring job, a difficult board member, nukes, logging, a piece of legislation, or any number of conflicts or problems. Such reactive visions may indeed solve certain problems. But they produce very different results than John F. Kennedy's creative vision of "putting a man on the moon by the end of the decade," or Martin Luther King, Jr.'s vision of seeing a day when "men are judged . . . by the content of their character." Rather than getting rid of something, these visions focused on bringing something powerful and new into existence. This is the heart of true, enduring innovation.

- **It emphasizes the outcome rather than process.** Emmy maintained her focus on the tree on the other side of the canyon, and the discovery of new worlds that it symbolized. The process for actually *getting* to the tree only occurred to her later. Remember, because a vision is a statement of end results—a declaration or image that literally brings a new reality into existence—the *how* of reaching the vision may not be immediately evident. The mechanism for realizing your vision is likely to emerge as you maintain a creative orientation, focusing purely on the vision. For many, the challenge is to have faith in the natural process of change, and in your own intuitive ability to adapt and learn in the pursuit of your vision. It's amazing how, when you focus on the outcome, the way to get there very often reveals itself.

- **It is something you want, simply because you want it.** When talking to people of deep personal mastery, one quickly senses that they are operating from a place that is profound, mysterious, and for some even spiritual. Lenny approached this inner place when he said, "I can't answer why I want this. I want it because I want it."

For Your Reflection:

- Imagine that your life exists exactly the way that you want it to be—regardless of what you believe is actually possible. What do you see?

- Think about or meditate on your "desired future state." Ask yourself: "What is it I want to create?" If you were to allow yourself to dream without boundaries, what can you see yourself bringing into existence that would be energizing and joyful? What is a vision you would feel passionate about?

Purpose and Vision Together

Purpose and vision are most powerful when they are aligned. For example, Lenny's *vision* was to become a motivational speaker. This was compatible with his *purpose* of helping the lemmings find joy in community. Likewise, Emmy's *purpose* of asking questions that open up bigger worlds and new ways of seeing resulted in her first *vision* of reaching the other side of the cliff. Once she achieved that vision, she defined another one, also consistent with her purpose: the construction of a pair of wings that could take her to even newer and more distant worlds.

When aligned, purpose and vision bring extraordinary clarity to decision-making. The right path just seems to reveal itself (as Lenny experienced when he suddenly realized he must leave the N.O. L.E.A.P.S.). I spoke with a woman who embodies this powerful relationship between vision and purpose quite nicely. I asked the woman, who is a child and family therapist as well as a gifted public speaker, what her life's purpose might be. "I believe it is to illuminate," she said.

"To illuminate?" I asked.

"It's interesting," she explained, "how often the clients in my counseling practice use images of lighthouses to describe me or thank me. It's a metaphor that keeps coming up in my life. Even my name means *bright-shining star*. But the metaphor is accurate. I am happiest when I am helping people see important truths in their lives and relationships that they could not see before."

"So how do your counseling practice and your public speaking fit into this?" I asked, since I had assumed that these activities were of the highest importance to her.

She thought for a moment. "They are merely ways to help me illuminate. I will pursue them only as long as they are consistent with that purpose." Today, this woman has completely left her counselling practice to be a full-time mother. An easy choice, she says, as she will be spending the next years joyfully illuminating the way for her child.

The more clearly we understand our purpose and visions, the more intentional we can become in virtually any activity in any arena of life. One colleague, who sees her purpose as "building learning capabilities in other people," experiences increased clarity in even the mundane tasks of her life: "Now, I almost never enter a meeting or a conversation without first identifying what it is that I'm trying to accomplish with that interaction, and testing whether it is consistent with my purpose," she said.

For Your Reflection:

- If you identified a vision in the above section, ask yourself: How might this vision relate to my life purpose? To discern this, ask yourself, "Why do I want this? What would it get me?" and write down your answer. Then ask again: "Why do I want this?" Again, write down your answer. Continue digging deeper in this way as you begin to deepen your awareness of your purpose.

Tension Maintenance

If all we had to do was to identify what we wanted and then wait for creative tension to draw us to the goal, our experience of life would be very different than it is. But as most of us can attest, it doesn't happen quite that easily.

The truth is, creative tension is a precarious balance. It is all too easy to slip out of the creative-tension structure and become stuck in a reactive orientation. Recall what happened to Emmy just as she was riding the wind over the canyon. She took her eye off of her desired future state, and instead became painfully aware of herself and her place in the gap. This kind of self-sabotage is an experience that virtually everyone can identify with.

In his book *Synchronicity: The Inner Path of Leadership,* author Joseph Jaworski paints a vivid illustration of the elusive nature of focus. He describes how, while one day shooting skeet at a firing range, he entered into a state of intense hyper-focus. He was keenly attuned to his own posture, the feel of the gun, and the trajectory of each clay pigeon as it flew over the firing range. Totally lost in the moment, he hit the small, airborne targets, one after another. Suddenly, Jaworski realized that, with just one pigeon to go, he was on the verge of achieving a perfect score — and, in fact, a crowd of amazed onlookers had gathered around him. Anxious to achieve perfection and impress the crowd, he then took his final shot at the last clay pigeon—and missed.

Perhaps you have had the experience of being intensely immersed in an activity such as playing tennis, writing a poem, playing a musical piece, or designing a new work process, where the work suddenly feels effortless—as if it were happening by itself and you were merely a participant. When you are truly in a state of creative tension, it works. There's no need to control the process. In fact, it can be an exhilarating experience as the tension seeks resolution and draws you to your desired future state. If you do find yourself struggling, or if achieving the vision just seems too hard, that's a good sign that your attention has shifted away from your vision and you have entered a reactive orientation.

At such moments, it is important to reenter the creative orientation by focusing on the two central states of awareness: *Where do I want to be? And where am I now?*

My desired future state   *My current reality*

Let's explore that second question a little more. As you pursue your vision, it is important to constantly and honestly assess your current reality. Where are you now? What obstacles are impeding your progress? What challenges must you be aware of? What hidden beliefs or mental models do you hold that are disabling the creative-tension structure? Surfacing these issues diffuses much of their hidden power.

You combat the crippling effects of your hidden beliefs by continually bringing them into the open, and by acknowledging them as part of your current reality. Too often, we respond as Lenny did: "Don't listen to those negative feelings ... they'll ruin everything." (Hear the reactive orientation creeping in?) But rather than trying to ignore something that felt bad, Emmy remained true to her creative orientation: "Well, at least now I know how hard this really is." She acknowledged her current reality, and this allowed her to refocus on her vision.

This is a very difficult thing to do. It requires courage, constant self-reflection, and an unyielding commitment to the truth of your current reality, and to your vision. (For those who find the process overwhelming, it may also require the help of a counselor or coach.) This pursuit of self-knowledge in service of our vision is a choice we must make every moment of every day.

For Your Reflection:

- What beliefs do you hold about yourself that prevent you from achieving your visions?

- What aspects of your current reality must you acknowledge in order to begin moving toward your vision?

- What structures, relationships, and contexts can you create or participate in that will help you stay aligned with your vision?

"What Do I Want to Create?"

So, who are you? What unique gift do you bring to the world? What do you wish to create?

When you begin to consider these questions, you embark on a rich journey of self-discovery that is never complete. Every day, you become a little clearer about your unique purpose (why you exist) and your vision (how your purpose is manifested in the things you wish to bring into existence).

We tend to think of creators as sculptors, musicians, and poets. But the act of creation is really about imagining something that you care about and bringing it into existence. In this way, you are a creator and your lifetime is your canvas, awaiting your inspiration and calling out for your participation. To become an active participant in shaping your own life is one of the great privileges of living.

Like all journeys, this one begins with a first step. To take this step, ask yourself:

Why am I here?
And what is it I wish to create?

80

Questions for Group Discussion

The Lemming Dilemma explores the principles of personal mastery at an individual level. However, these principles are equally important at the organizational level. To begin considering the organizational applications of personal mastery, discuss the following questions in your team, department, or company.

- How can your organization better encourage the practice of personal mastery? What systems and structures could be put in place to enable people to pursue this discipline?

- What is your organization's purpose?

- What are some *visions* that your organization has had? How are these visions consistent or inconsistent with your organization's purpose?

- Give an example of a time your organization operated from a *reactive* orientation. Give an example of a time it operated from a *creative* orientation. What were the results in each case?

- Can you think of a time that your organization enabled the creative-tension structure? (That is, it focused on a compelling *desired future state* while honestly acknowledging its *current reality*.) Was the organization able to maintain its focus on the desired future state? What were the ultimate results? Why?

Acknowledgments

Simplicity is complex. Written, then rewritten, then rewritten many more times, *The Lemming Dilemma* is the product of a deep learning journey that prompted an approach to the most sacred areas of my own life. Such a journey is greatly eased through the guidance of a mentor; during the development of this manuscript, I was fortunate to work closely with three:

- *Renee Moorefield*, of WisdomWorks, is a gifted coach and confidante who is a guide for my own flights over the cliff and across the canyon;

- *LouAnn Daly* is a rare woman of deep purpose. A great coach because of what she *says*; a true mentor because of what she *is*;

- *Teresa Hogan* was there at the beginning of this journey, more than a decade ago, and continues to be my trusted guide and friend.

The development of this story was informed, in part, by a series of informal interviews with practitioners of the discipline of personal mastery. In the story, Lenny felt a "strange electricity" as he approached the holy ground of awareness. So did I as I spoke with and learned from these deeply aware people:

- *Susan Gerke* of Gerke Consulting; *Amy White* of The Coca-Cola Learning Consortium; *Joe Simonet* of The Coca-Cola Learning Consortium.

Special thanks to the following reviewers for their insightful and important feedback on early drafts of the manuscript:

- *Robert Fritz*, of Technologies for Creating; *Julie Hayden* of The Coca-Cola Learning Consortium; *Jeff Jones* of T. Rowe Price; and *Marilyn Paul*, of Marilyn Paul and Associates.

As always, a big debt goes to the Pegasi—particularly my warm, wonderful editor, *Lauren Keller Johnson*. While the rest of the world works, we spend our hours pontificating about sheep, cavepeople, and lemmings—and debating what we would do if we were them. What a great job.

To my wife *Robbie*, who illuminates. Any inspiration that is to be found in this book is merely channeled through me; you are my source.

And, finally, to my daughter *Emory*: This one had to be for you. You help me know who I am and why I'm here. Have faith, for a wonderful purpose is waiting to unfold before you.

Suggested Further Reading

———•———

- *The Path of Least Resistance* by Robert Fritz. (An important contribution to the field of personal mastery, and the source of many of the models and concepts explored in *The Lemming Dilemma*.)

- *The Inner Game of Tennis* by W. Timothy Gallwey. (A book that is about much more than sports psychology. Read it for important insights into the nature of learning, even if you have never picked up a tennis racket.)

- *Flow: The Psychology of Optimal Experience* by Mihaly Csikszentmihalyi. (A lucid and exciting exploration of meaningful experiences. The author's approach is smart and scientific, but very readable.)

- *Man's Search for Meaning* by Viktor Frankl. (From his horrifying experiences during the Nazi holocaust, Frankl developed his logotherapy, in which people may derive meaning in their lives by focusing on a compelling future state.)

- *Synchronicity: The Inner Path of Leadership* by Joe Jaworski. (A moving and personal account of the search for meaning by a revered organizational leader.)

- *The Fifth Discipline* by Peter Senge. (The seminal book on the five disciplines of organizational learning. Includes a significant discussion of the discipline of personal mastery.)

Other Titles by Pegasus Communications

Learning Fables
Outlearning the Wolves: Surviving and Thriving in a Learning Organization
Shadows of the Neanderthal: Illuminating the Beliefs That Limit Our Organizations

The Pegasus Workbook Series
Systems Archetype Basics: From Story to Structure
Systems Thinking Basics: From Concepts to Causal Loops

The "Billibonk" Jungle Mysteries
Billibonk & the Thorn Patch   *Frankl's "Thorn Patch" Fieldbook*
Billibonk & the Big Itch   *Frankl's "Big Itch" Fieldbook*

Human Dynamics
Human Dynamics: A New Framework for Understanding People and Realizing the Potential in Our Organizations

The Pegasus Anthology Series
Reflections on Creating Learning Organizations
Managing the Rapids: Stories from the Forefront of the Learning Organization
The New Workplace: Transforming the Character and Culture of Our Organizations
Organizational Learning at Work: Embracing the Challenges of the New Workplace
Making It Happen: Stories from Inside the New Workplace

Newsletters
THE SYSTEMS THINKER™
LEVERAGE®: News and Ideas for the Organizational Learner

The Innovations in Management Series
Concise, practical volumes on systems thinking and organizational learning tools, principles, and applications.

84